An
Assortment
Of Animals

A Children's Poetry Anthology

by The Writers' Loft
Authors & Illustrators

To all assortments of people who have said,
"Here, read this poem."

Published by
The Writers' Loft Press, Sherborn, MA
thewritersloft.org

An Assortment of Animals: A Children's Poetry Anthology
Kristen Wixted, HG Kelly, Editors
Sally Hinkley, Priscilla Alpaugh, Art Advisors
Cover art copyright © 2018 Brian Lies
Book Design copyright © 2018 Doreen Buchinski

Second Edition
10 9 8 7 6 5 4 3 2
copyright © The Writers' Loft Press, 2018

ISBN 9780998317212
For information about permission to reproduce selections from this book
please write to:
writersloftma@gmail.com.

THE WRITERS' LOFT

Table of Contents

Where's the Barracuda?

by Jane Yolen

Enigma, chameleon, a puzzle,
a mask.
There in the ocean in motionless
bask,

barracuda dissembles and hides in the
greenery,
disguising his length in the sea bottom
scenery.

Illustrated by Brian Lies

Consider the Slug

by Brian Lies

We're reclusive, we're reviled.
But our manner? Gentle, mild!
No fang or poison, speed or size
causes us to terrorize.

No—that shudder, that disgust?
It's you that blundered into us!
A thoughtless reach or barefoot stride,
you stumble on us where we hide.

If you pause, it's pretty sweet,
our oozy engineering feat.
We lay our tracks down as we go,
like a train, but silent, slow.

The worst we do—no devil's dance—
is savaging some garden plants.
So leave us be, and off we'll glide
on our slo-mo Slip 'n' Slide.

Illustrated by Brian Lies

A Crash of Rhinos—Hold the Tutus

by Audrey Day-Williams

Of things that you will never see, least-likeliest by far:

A toe-shoed-wearing rhino with her hoof upon the barre.

It's not that odd-toed ungulates in tutus are cliché,

Their three-toed hooves don't fit the shoes you wear to dance ballet.

It's hard to pull on ballet tights when all you've got are toes,

That's why they dance in birthday suits *(that means they don't wear clothes).*

There's rumor of an ancient herd who really loved to dance,

With wild abandon on the plains, they'd twirl and spin and prance.

A rhino group is called a crash—the name is no mistake,

Their legendary dances would leave chaos in their wake.

But sigh, that's just a fairytale passed down from long ago;

Rhinoceros don't dance or twirl; they're fans of moving slow.

But some nights still, I dream the moon becomes a disco ball,

And underneath it rhinos dance with nothing on at all.

6   *Illustrated by Priscilla Alpaugh*

Each is Great

by Dave Pasquantonio

Each of the cats thought that he was the best.
As you'll learn, each in turn
tried to one-up the rest.

Cheetah said, "Dudes, I'm so quick and so fast.
Any race, any place.
You would *all* come in last."

Lion said, "Doubt it. Have you heard me roar?
You will shake. You will quake.
I'm too much to ignore."

Leopard said, "Boring. Hey, check out my spots!
They razzle. They dazzle.
I've got lots and lots."

Tiger said, "Please. You think spots are so great?
You're a fool. *Stripes* are cool.
It's not up for debate."

The smack talk continued. They acted like brats.
Let's be straight. Each is great.
We don't need catty cats!

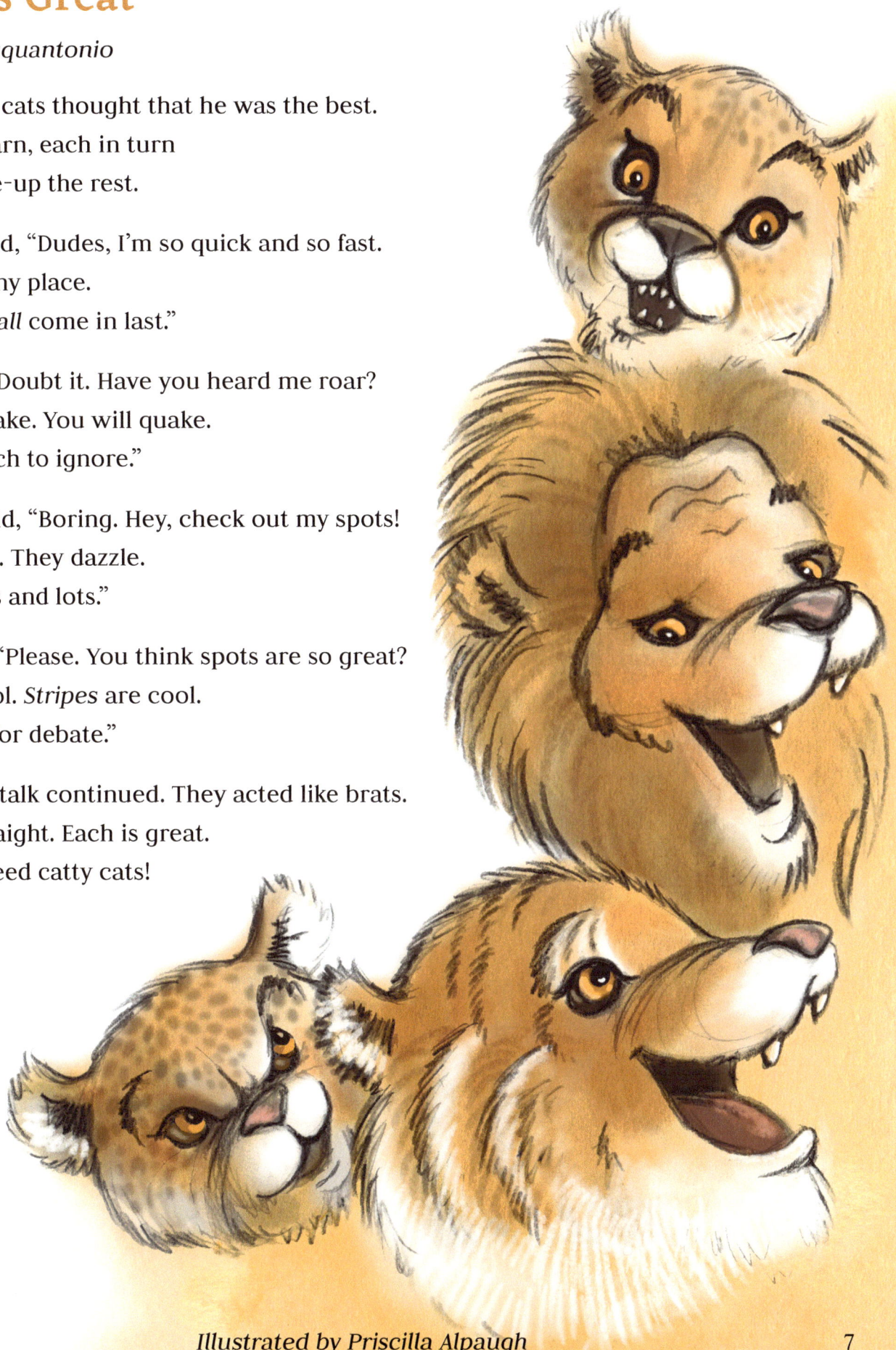

Illustrated by Priscilla Alpaugh

The Centipede

by Ellen Cohen

If you want to please a centipede
I know just what she'd choose–
A shopping expedition
To buy some pairs of shoes.

What do you think she'd like to wear
On her hundred little feet?
Slippers when she's in her house?
Sandals on the street?

High heels for the runway?
Flip flops for the beach?
Tap shoes, toe shoes for the stage?
(She'd need 50 pairs of each.)

If she wants a set of sneakers
Different colors, different brands,
Be prepared to tie the laces
As she hasn't any hands.

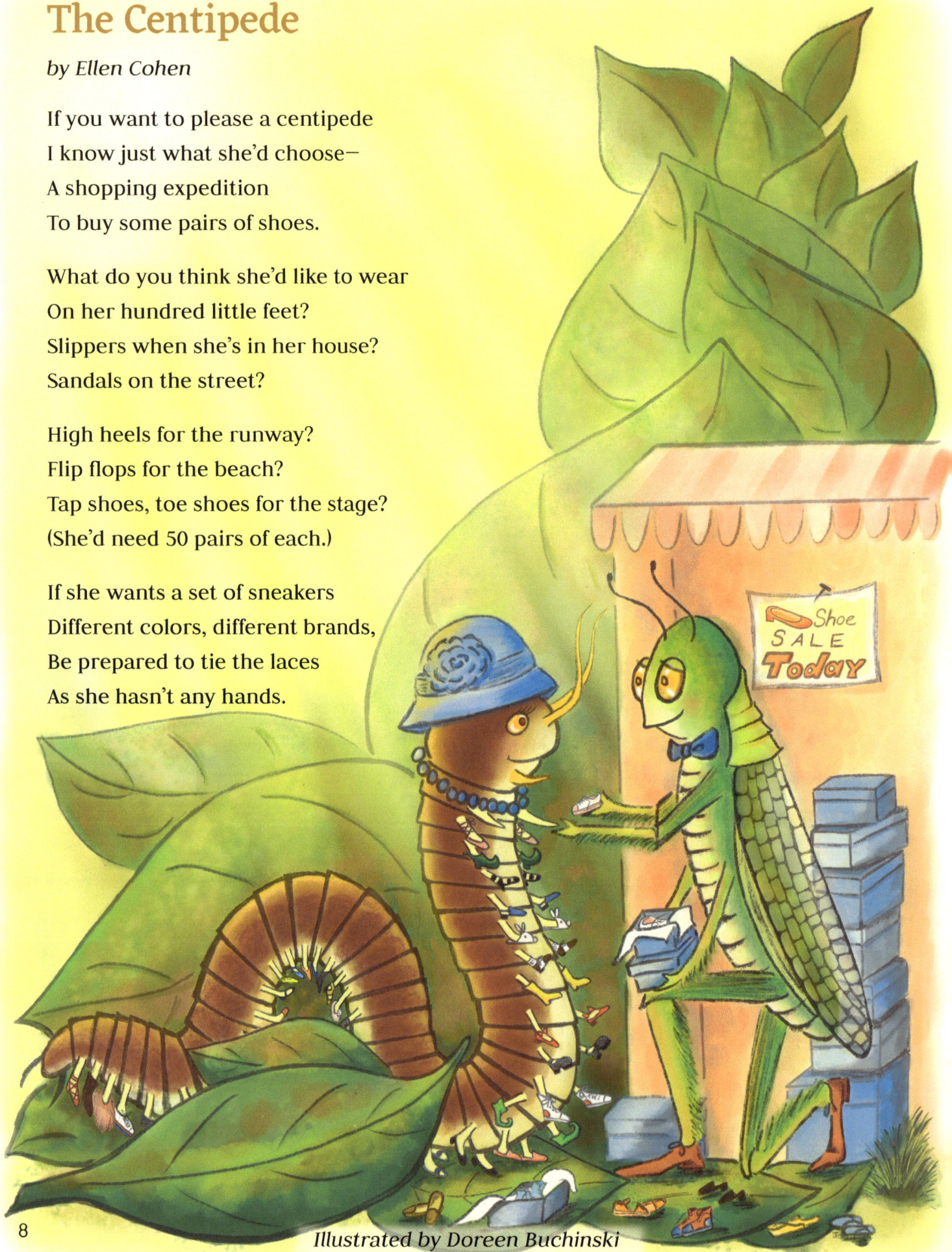

8

Illustrated by Doreen Buchinski

Baby Giraffe

by Charlotte Sheer

When baby giraffe
Arrives as a calf,
He weighs over
One hundred pounds.
The Mama cow stands,
While the little one lands,
In her shadow and
Onto the ground!
With hardly a sound,
All spotted and brown,
A tangle of legs in a heap,
Within just an hour,
The young six-foot tower
Is nuzzled and coaxed
To his feet.

Illustrated by Doreen Buchinski

Great Blue Heron

by Kristen Wixted

Inconspicuous,
Supremely precise.
Heron will coil,
Heron will spoil
The day
Of his prey.

Indiscernible,
Rarely exposed.
Heron will hide,
Call to his bride.
He squawks
When he talks.

Unremarkable,
Plumage is gray.
Heron will stand
Still as the sand.
You're close ...
Up he goes.

Illustrated by Priscilla Alpaugh

Flamingo Morning

by Jane Yolen

She's pink, so pink,
From head to toes,
And like a sunrise,
She arose.

A Flamboyance

by Kristen Wixted

Flamingos, when stretching their wings to the side
Are shorter in height than their wingspan is wide.
Flamingos lay eggs that they hide in a mound,
Flamingos hatch chicks any time, all year round.
The babies have feathers of gray or of white,
Which then turn vermilion or pink, aptly bright.
The pink is flamboyant−such a strong hue
Is not often chosen by me or by you.
But flamingos, they like it, they like it a lot.
They don't really care if you like it or not.
Flamingos aren't bashful or feeble of brain,
In fact they are brilliant and frightfully vain.

Illustrated by Priscilla Alpaugh

Monarch

by Sandy Budiansky

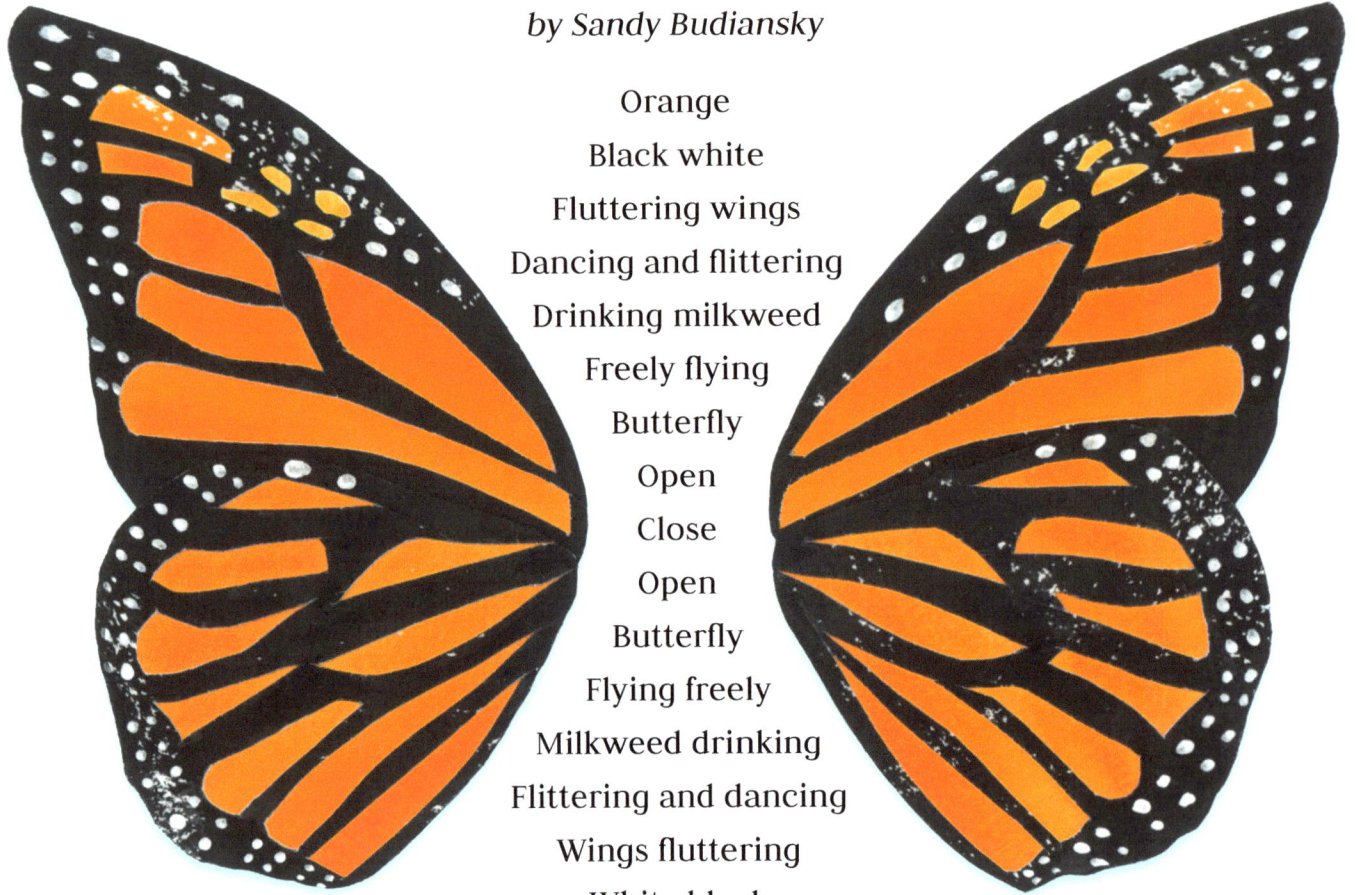

Orange
Black white
Fluttering wings
Dancing and flittering
Drinking milkweed
Freely flying
Butterfly
Open
Close
Open
Butterfly
Flying freely
Milkweed drinking
Flittering and dancing
Wings fluttering
White black
Orange

Illustrated by Marty Lapointe-Malchik

Snowbirds

by Marty Lapointe-Malchik

Don't worry, Grandpa.
I put seeds on the ground.
Plenty of juncos still come around.

Don't worry, Grandpa.
I hear chirps in the tree.
They see me coming. *Chicka-dee-dee.*

Don't worry, Grandpa.
I spot glimpses of red.
Far from the house your cardinals are fed.

Don't worry, Grandpa.
Take your time by the sea.
I'll feed your birds 'til you fly back to me.

Illustrated by Marty Lapointe-Malchik

Walk a Mile in my Plume

by Heather Kelly

Crystalline eyes fan out behind me,
Three long years they took to grow.
"Proud" is the name you call my beauty.
I have no say in what I tow.

Quivering plumes sing out my story.
Too low for human ears, the sound.
"Shake your tail feathers," mocks my glory.
My mate cares not, and I am found.

Shimmering train attracts my enemy.
Six feet of drag, for sure, I'm tough.
Taking my flight, flapping extremity,
Still you say I strut my stuff.

Dripping my plumes and molting goodbye.
Feathers of color; green, silver, blue.
Without a thought, a pause, a cry,
I give a few of my jewels to you.

14   *Illustrated by Jodie Apeseche*

Dragonfly—
Master of Flight

by Megan Litwin

Of all the things that fly above—
Rocket, dragon, black fly, dove,

There is but one so strong yet light
Who dazzles with a dance of flight.

Speedy shimmer, zig, zag, zip,
Forward, backward, hover, dip.

A paper airplane, wings of glass,
Bestowing luck on all who pass.

Illustrated by Jodie Apeseche

15

Lampreys

by Luke Hargrave

Lampreys grab a passing fish, and when the fish finds out,

It tries to get them off but can't. Oh my the poor, poor trout.

Their rows of spiny teeth hold on, their tongues strike without rest,

The lampreys are true killers; they are more than just a pest!

The lampreys are not picky, they'll eat most anything,

As long as it has flesh and blood, they'll leave a creepy ring.

Be thankful that they have dull minds—they're known to bite on rocks

For respite from a tiring swim; good thing they're shaped like socks!

Illustrated by Robert Thibeault

Jellyfish

by Robin Brett Wechsler

Umbrella-shaped jelly
not a fish and not smelly seeking
krill to eat, I pulsate to a beat—along
the ocean floor until a wave
drives me ashore.

Sting!	Or
sun-dry	is
what	I
might	do.
Oh!	Wait.
A surge	draws
me	back—
Phew!	

Illustrated by Robert Thibeault

The Superb Blue-crowned Motmot

by Jane Sutton

It is not hard to spot-spot
The superb Blue-crowned Motmot.
They're the brightest of blue-blue
And loud Whoop-Whoops they do-do.
Plus you never could fail-fail
To be wowed by that tail-tail!

Illustrated by Doreen Buchinski

Hipster Hamster

by Josh Funk

Hipster Hamster hurried home.
The day had been a bust.
The protest had been canceled.
His bike was caked in rust.

His avocado toast was burnt.
His flat white stained his vest.
His mustache didn't curl right.
He felt a tad depressed.

The worst day of his life, no doubt—
He wished he could erase it.
At last he reached his home sweet home
Inside his parents' basement.

Illustrated by Doreen Buchinski

A Pangolin's Tale

by Jodie Apeseche

Pangolin is hungry and searching for food.
She sticks out her tongue but not to be rude.
It's as long as her body, can reach far and wide,
Slurping up ants, with her nose as her guide.

Pangolin's unique—she's covered in scales,
Made up of keratin, just like our nails.
She looks like an artichoke or pinecone on legs.
And because she's a mammal, she doesn't lay eggs.

Giving her baby a piggyback ride,
She hobbles back home to her burrow dug wide.
Together they snuggle—a ball curled up tight,
Their breath a mere whisper, enclosed by the night.

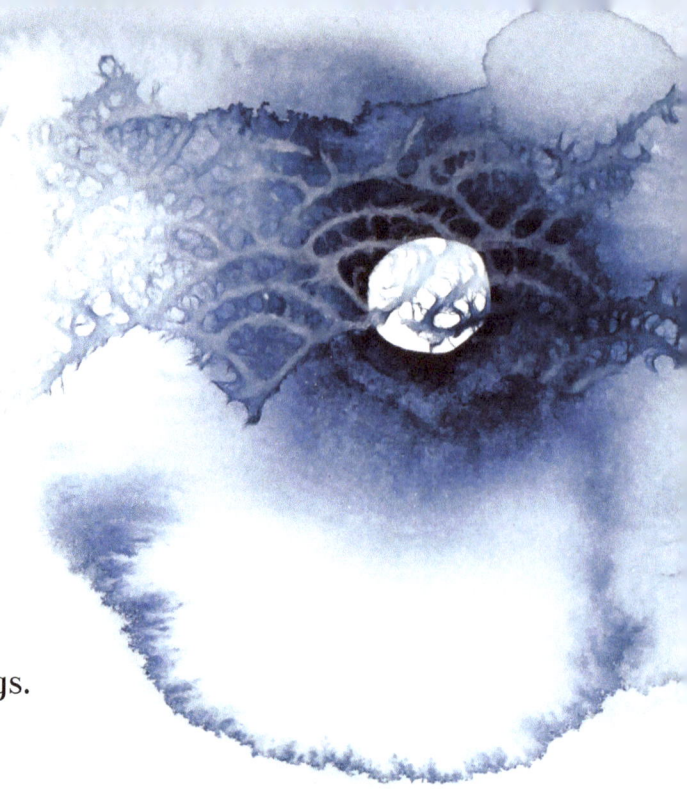

Illustrated by Jodie Apeseche

White on Brown

by Jane Kohuth

There by the rocks
just behind that brush
under the drowned trees
they pop
like daubs of whitest white on brown.
The swans stay through winter
in the wetlands,
waiting.
Now one is bottoms up
wiggling tail feathers,
while the other lifts her face
to the spring sun.

Illustrated by Jodie Apeseche

21

Get to Know Grizzly Bear

by Audrey Day-Williams

Exploring in the woods one day, I came across a bear.
She saw that I looked terrified and grumbled, "Life's not fair.
I feel that I'm misunderstood, perhaps because my teeth—
I've got so many up above, so many underneath.
I'm scared of you, you're scared of me, and why? Because my claws?
Don't judge a bear until you've walked a mile in their paws."

I grabbed my pad, my favorite pen, and right there on the spot
I interviewed that grizzly bear. And boy, I learned a lot.

I asked her what bears do for fun, perhaps they like to bowl?
She sadly said, she tried it once, but has no thumbs for holes.
I thought, well maybe shooting hoops, since grizzlies are so tall?
She laughed as if I should have known that bears can't jump at all.
"Do bears like making angels then, in freshly-fallen snow?
Jogging? Dodge ball? Do you ski? How 'bout a Broadway show?"

She shook her head; I sighed and asked, "What *do* bears like to do?"
She toothy-grinned. "We like to lunch ... after an interview."

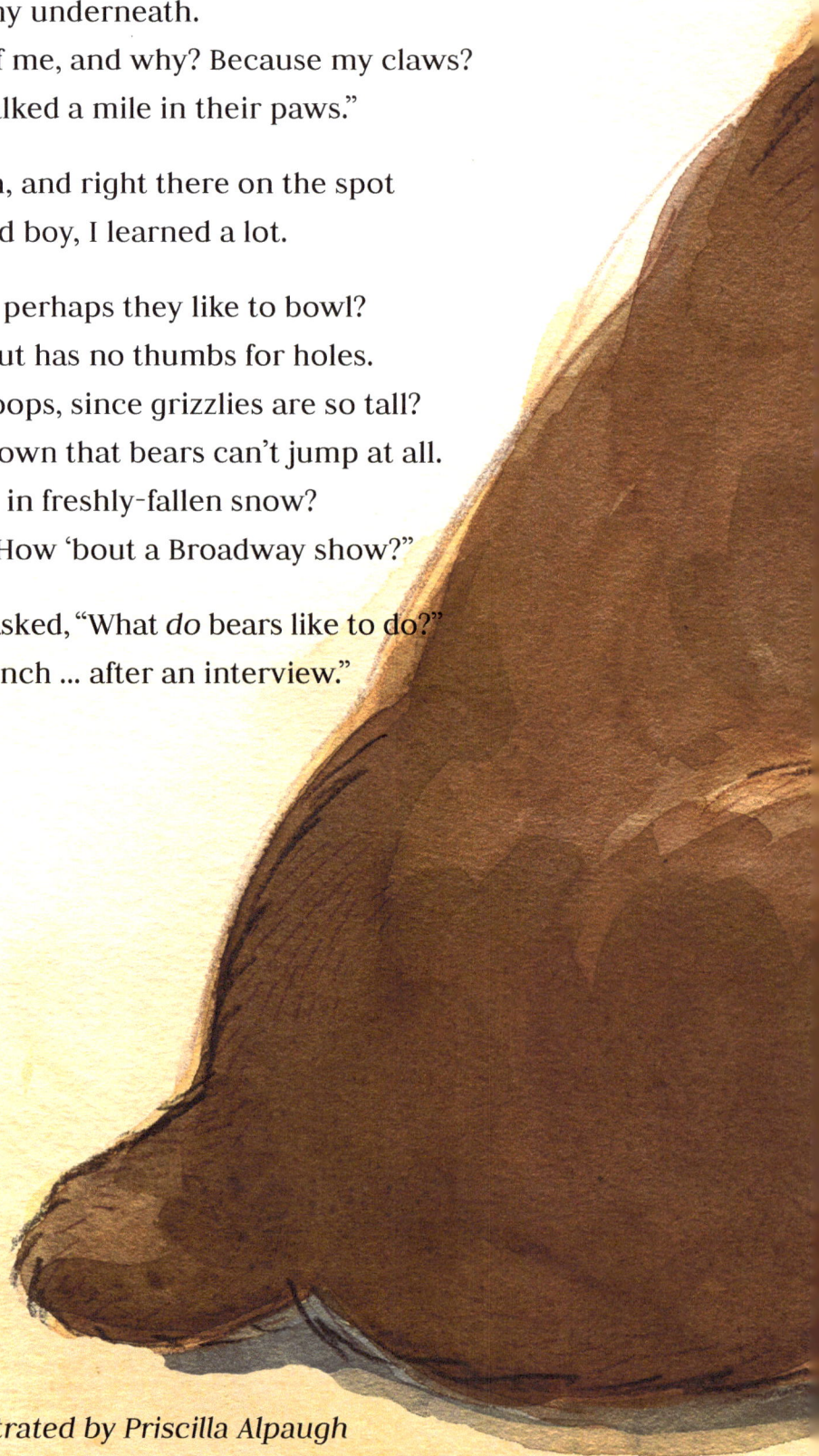

Illustrated by Priscilla Alpaugh

S'il Vous Plaît

by Cathleen Stenquist

I wish a fish were on my dish,
filet with sauce mornay
and lobster claws
with buttery sauce;
a feline feast soirée.

I dream of tuna, seared and pink,
of scallop ratatouille;
grilled trout filets
with warm béarnaise,
mussels steamed and chewy.

No cultured palate, quite this fine,
allows a canned ragoût.
Eww!
But should there be no haute cuisine ...
A tuna melt will do.

24   *Illustrated by Robert Thibeault*

Dog Gone

by Pam Vaughan

I'm finished. I'm done. I'm running away.
It's over. I've had it. No reason to stay.

Can't bury the bones, or sit on the bed.
Can't bark through the night. They groan when I shed.

No stealing their shoes, no gnawing on socks,
No growling at strangers, no digging up rocks.

Can't eat when I want ... it doesn't make sense.
Stuck out in this yard, surrounded by fence.

It's time to move on; to go it alone.
I'll do as I please when I'm out on my own.

Although ...

I do like the walks, and the treats, and the pats,
Keeping vermin away, and chasing the cats.

They NEED a great watch dog; I keep the yard clear,
Without me, the riff-raff would settle in here.

I guess that I'll stay just a little bit more,
HEY, SQUIRREL ... it's MY home, I'll show you the door!

Illustrated by Robert Thibeault

Friend or Food

by Deborah O'Brien

The anteater had spent the day without a thing to eat,
Until he spied one little ant and said, "I found a treat.

Your limbs are crisp and crunchy, your body tasty, too.
With endless possibilities, I'm not sure what to do.

On pizza you'd be tangy with a little bit of dirt.
Perhaps I'll dip you in hot fudge and save you for dessert."

"Dear Sir," the insect pointed out, "I beg to disagree.
My arms are thin, my torso lean; there isn't much to me.

But you, my friend, are grand in size with such a massive snout.
I bet that you would suck me up but then just spit me out.

A mammal with your appetite, this snack won't satisfy.
So, shake my hand, agree to part, and we'll just say goodbye."

The ant bowed low with confidence, assured he'd made his case.
Then looked his foe right in the eye, a smile upon his face.

The giant paused. He liked this ant and what he had to say.
But it was late; Anteater shrugged and ate him anyway.

Illustrated by Deborah O'Brien

A Funny–Looking Bird

by Charlotte Sheer

An albatross known as the Gooney:
Long wings make him look buffoony.
He takes flight rather wobbly,
And crash lands quite hobbly—
An ornithological looney.

Illustrated by Deborah O'Brien

Turkey Vultures

by Jane Yolen

Turkey vultures can smell you,
Can tell you
Are dead.
Their necks have no feathers.
Cold weathers
They dread.

Their black vulture cousins,
By dozens,
Can't smell.
So they hang out with others,
Like brothers,
Who tell

All the dead from the living,
Forgiving
the quick.
Here come the vultures;
I must be
Real sick.

Illustrated by Joy Nelkin Wieder

Araneae

by Kari Allen

The climber
The spinner
The weaver
The corner decorator
The watcher
The waiter
The trapper
The ever vigilant spider

A Platypus looks like a Platypus Should

by Dave Pasquantonio

Duck says my bill means I must be a duck
(But one who is not feather-y).

Beaver asks why I don't ever build dams
(Since my flat tail is so beaver-y).

Swan thinks we're twins 'cause we both have webbed feet
(So a swan is the thing I must be).

Turtle says since I lay eggs like she does,
I'm a turtle (so obviously).

All of my friends make some very good points,
But they're all incorrect (as you'll see).

A platypus looks like a platypus should,
(And that's what I love about me).

Illustrated by Joy Nelkin Wieder

The Prickly Porcupine

by Bonnie Gold

You may wear a winter coat
of soft and fluffy down;
a porcupine is wrapped in quills
it carries all year round.

The quills don't seem to bother him
but I can't really see,
how on his pointy mattress
he can sleep contentedly.

Those quills are his protection,
needle-sharp and spiny,
daring all, "I may be small—
but, buddy, just you try me!"

Illustrated by Deborah O'Brien

Wolverines

by Elaine D'Alessandro

Wandering ground hunters stocky and strong
Observant and aggressive in silent pursuit through
Layers of snow with crampon-like paws.
Voraciously sniffing before
Emitting a growling and bone crushing bite.
Rabbits and elk, foxes and moose find it
Impossible to avoid their powerful jaws
Nabbing and gnawing
Each creature's neck
Satisfying the wolverine's carnivorous ways.

Illustrated by Robert Thibeault

Heavy Feathers in the Sky

by Caitlin Kelly

The moon illuminated as if by wand
The night, the owl, an unbreakable bond.

Her shining eyes do not have to look high
The mix of blue and purple, the dazzling sky.

Those magical feathers, heavier than bone
Her long awaited screech well undertone.

At daybreak she nestles her head close to wing
Her eyes barely open 'til what next will bring.

Illustrated by Joy Nelkin Wieder

Pigeons

by Sally Hinkley

High above idling motors,
pigeons swap stories, nodding and cooing,
balancing
side-by-side along a bobbing wire
like iridescent beads on silvery strands
with stripes of pewter and slate,
emerald green and amethyst quills
that shimmer and sparkle in the morning sun.

Illustrated by Sally Hinkley

Tracing the Lines

by Sally Hinkley

If you trace the lines on an elephant's back,
The hours may pass, so bring a good snack.
Maybe some grapes? Or a juicy, ripe pear?
And whatever you do, remember to share.

Be careful of where the curvy lines stray.
They can trail off to places that just aren't okay.
Say your excuse me's and move right along,
Time will rush by if you hum a good song.

But those wrinkles may turn and go on forever
Like rivers on maps that all merge together.
Don't think that you're lost or gone the wrong way,
Keep following the intricate ripples of grey.

Down and then up to the top of a peak,
Look at the wonder, so kind and unique.
Oh, where did we land? It's just the right place,
In front of that beautiful elephant's face!

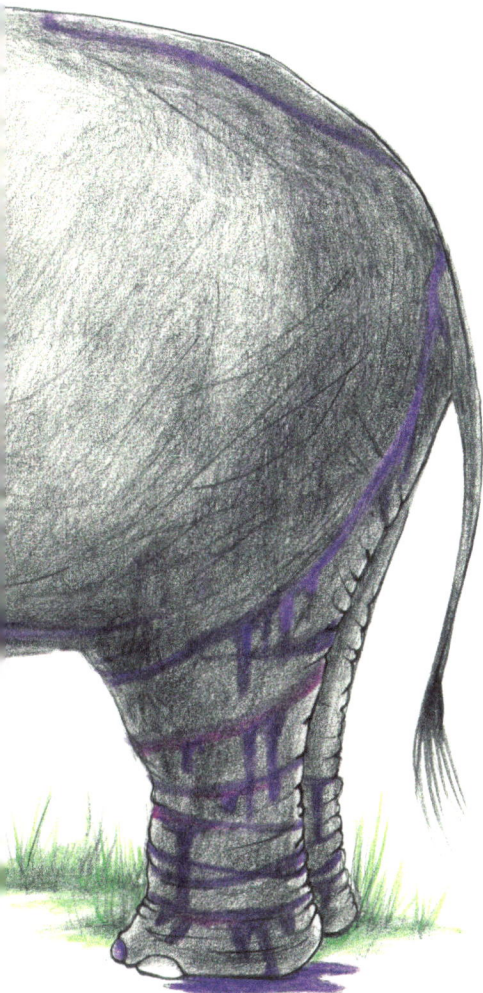

Not Even the Black Flag

by Jane Yolen

That old mockingbird
Pirating songs
Until he has made them his own.

Without a treasure chest,
Or eye patch,
Not even the black flag,

He sails across the garden,
The stolen songs
Heavy in his beak

His camouflage is gray as air.
Be careful he doesn't steal
The bells of your phone,

The sigh from your mouth,
A smack of your lips,
The beat of your heavy heart.

Illustrated by Priscilla Alpaugh

Toes to Hooves

by Hayley Barrett

We're sometimes known as eohippus.
Though modern horses far outstrip us

In size and in acceleration,
Their might stands on our slight foundation

Of tiny toes—more than a dozen.
For we're the horse's oldest cousin.

Through evolution, we slowly changed.
Once numerous digits rearranged.

Four mid-toes began to dominate
Until they—our hooves!—bore all the weight.

The others? Each shrank to nearly nil,
Vestigial, yet evident still.

Toes-to-hooves, a key adaptation,
Reveals our paleo-relation.

So remember, fossil record shows,
From eohippus—the horse arose.

Illustrated by Priscilla Alpaugh

Mobile Home

by Helen Kampion

Travelin' everywhere—
Don't have to pack.
All that I need
Is right on my back.

Don't need a cave,
Don't need a nest,
Got my own house,
To snuggle and rest.

Pull in my toes,
Tuck in my head,
Cuddle on down,
In my very own bed.

Illustrated by Jodie Apeseche

Betta Fish

by Alice Carty Fulgione

Betta, Betta, Betta Fish,
Swimming proudly in your dish.

Will you fight a fish today?
No, not you, you want to play.

You prefer to swim alone,
Round and round a lava stone,

Fanning tail has prism hues,
Silvers, purples, reds, and blues.

Then you eat a shrimp or two,
Munching larvae, bloodworms, eww!!!

After eating, you can chill,
Silent, peaceful, floating, still,

Gazing at me, feeling bliss,
Blowing me a Betta kiss.

Illustrated by Jodie Apeseche

Bombus Pennsylvanicus

by Kari Allen

Fat bumble
Fuzzy bumble
Black and yellow buzzy bumble

Striped bumble
Busy bumble
Lazy loopy flier bumble

Rumbling bumble
Tumbling bumble
Bumbling bumble
Bumblebee

Conversation

by Jane Yolen

"Oh bee," says flower,
"as you go by me,
 I know that you'll
 electrify me."
"Oh flower," says bee,
"each minute, each hour,
 when I am in your
 potent power,

"I fizzle and fry.
 I buzz a lot.
 I know I want
 All that you've got."

Their conversation's
full and funny,
deeply moving—
very punny.

And they end up
with pots of honey.

Illustrated by Doreen Buchinski

Warnings to a Fawn

by Jane Yolen

Hush, child,
Do not move.
Be still as ice,
Silent as wind.
Dappled as trees.
Lie down in grass.

And, all disguised,
Let danger pass.

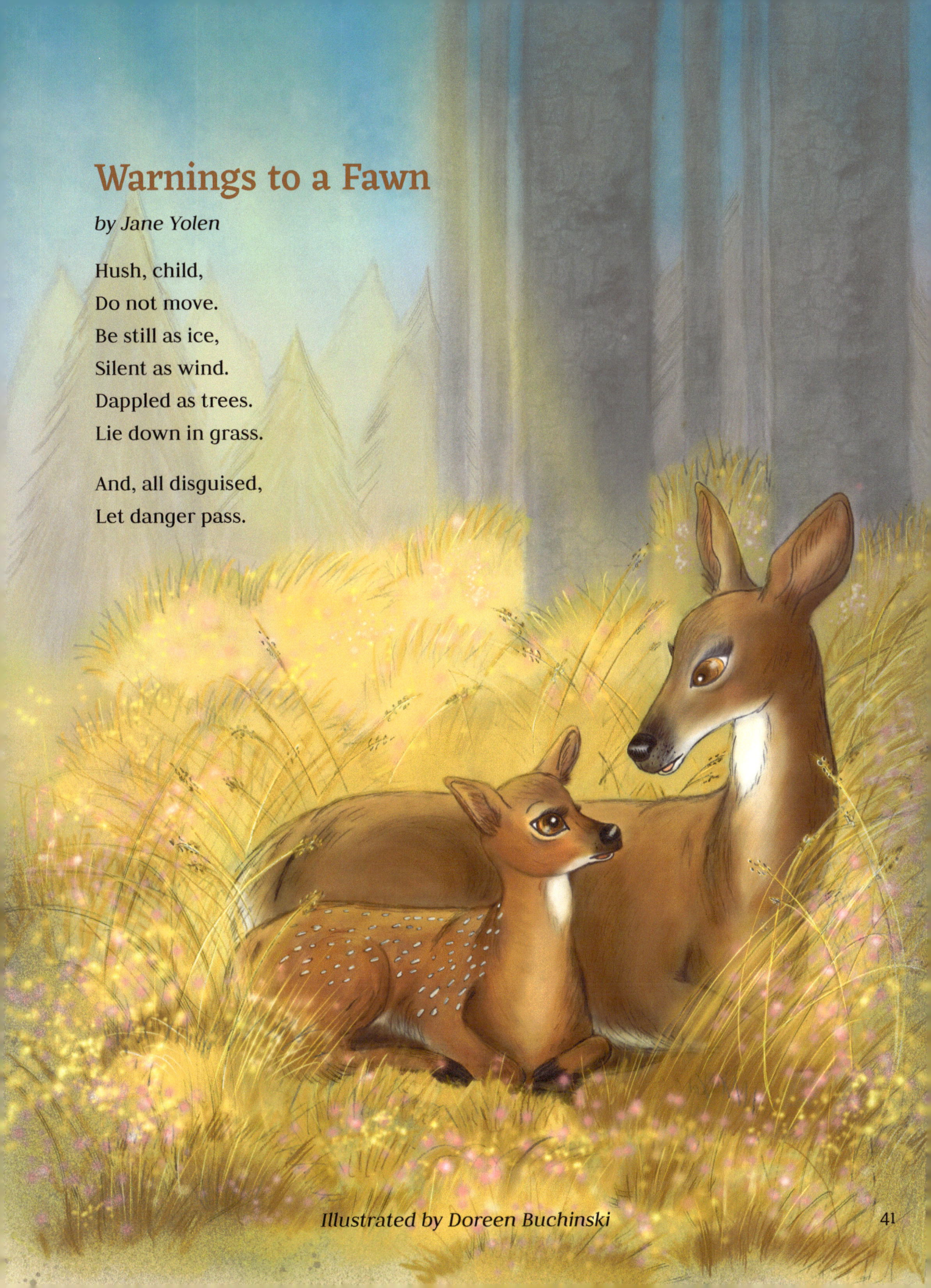

Illustrated by Doreen Buchinski

An Assortment of Animals:

Can you spot all these animals and other things in the book?

- **54** birds?
- **15** insects?
- **4** Scrabble tiles?
- **4** animals wearing hats?
- **1** lobster?
- **3** spiral shells?

- A pear? A can of paint?
- A sock? Bunny slippers?
- John Travolta (the animal version)?
- A swan-shaped cloud?
- A pair of eyes peeking out from under a tree?
- **3** flamingos holding the book you're reading?

An Assortment of Poems:

Can you find all these types of poems in this book?

1. An **Acrostic** poem's first or last letter in each line spells something out—a name, a thing, or a phrase.
2. A **Concrete** poem is one whose words create a picture of the subject of the poem.
3. **Free Verse** poems have no rules for words or punctuation. The author can do whatever is best to convey the idea of the poem!
4. A **Limerick** is a funny poem that follows the rhyme scheme AABBA.
5. A **Narrative** poem is one that tells a story of an event within its words.

Poetry can have rhyme schemes like ABAB or AABB, or others.
How many rhyme schemes do we have in our book?

An Assortment of Illustration Mediums:

The art mediums used by the artists in our book vary. Each type of art might make you feel different than the others. Our artists used these mediums: acrylic paint, watercolor, collages, colored pencil, pen and ink, and digital drawings and painting. **Can you spot some of them in the pages?**

We'll help you out. Can you find ...

- A digital dog?
- A pen and ink and watercolor porcupine?
- A peacock collage?
- An elephant with colored pencil lines?
- An acrylic barracuda?

An Assortment of Authors and Illustrators:

Authors and Illustrators need a place to creatively thrive—to learn their craft, to share knowledge, and to discuss story and art. For the assortment of authors and illustrators in this book, **The Writers' Loft** is that place. We have many members just starting out and many with established careers, but the most important thing is we're always enjoying each other's differences and learning and supporting each other. We hope you have a place like The Writers' Loft to thrive as an artist!

An Assortment of Readers:

We're so glad you found our book, and we'd love to hear from you!
Did any of the poems in the book inspire you to write your own poetry?
What was your favorite poem in our book? Your favorite illustration?
Have you tried any new mediums of art because a picture captured your imagination?
Let us know! Write to us at **writersloftma@gmail.com**.

For more information about the poems and illustrations in this book, or about writing poetry, go to **thewritersloft.org**.

www.ingramcontent.com/pod-product-compliance
Lightning Source LLC
Chambersburg PA
CBHW042017090426
42811CB00015B/1670

9 780998 317212